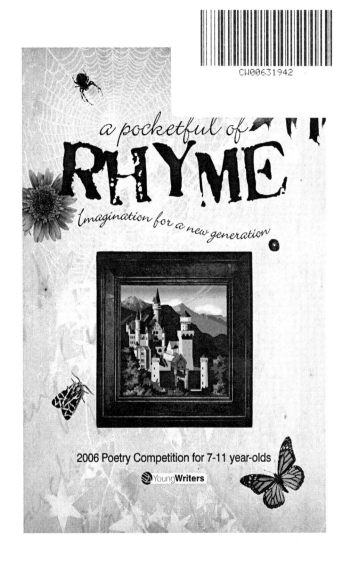

a pocketful of
RHYME

Imagination for a new generation

2006 Poetry Competition for 7-11 year-olds

YoungWriters

Poetic Voices From Wales
Edited by Gemma Hearn

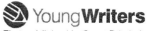 Young**Writers**

First published in Great Britain in 2006 by:
Young Writers
Remus House
Coltsfoot Drive
Peterborough
PE2 9JX
Telephone: 01733 890066
Website: www.youngwriters.co.uk

SB ISBN 1 84602 594 X

Foreword

Young Writers was established in 1991 and has been passionately devoted to the promotion of reading and writing in children and young adults ever since. The quest continues today. Young Writers remains as committed to the nurturing of poetic and literary talent as ever.

This year's Young Writers competition has proven as vibrant and dynamic as ever and we are delighted to present a showcase of the best poetry from across the UK and in some cases overseas. Each poem has been selected from a wealth of *A Pocketful Of Rhyme* entries before ultimately being published in this, our fourteenth primary school poetry series.

Once again, we have been supremely impressed by the overall quality of the entries we have received. The imagination, energy and creativity which has gone into each young writer's entry made choosing the poems a challenging and often difficult but ultimately hugely rewarding task - the general high standard of the work submitted ensured this opportunity to bring their poetry to a larger appreciative audience.

We sincerely hope you are pleased with this final collection and that you will enjoy *A Pocketful Of Rhyme Poetic Voices From Wales* for many years to come.

Contents

Billy Pringle (9)	32
Andrew Davies (9)	33
Oliver Hart (9)	34
Garion Brown (9)	35
Cameron Davies (9)	36
Mollie Allen (9)	37
Charlotte Pearce (9)	38
Ryan Jones (9)	39
Mary-Morgan Griffiths (9)	40
Lauren Jones (9)	41
Melanie Humphreys (8)	42
Alisha Bourne (8)	43
Sarah Williams (7)	44
Aaron Williams (7)	45
Rhys Sinnett	46
Seren Childs (8)	47
James Gretton (8)	48
Amie Baines (7)	49
Madeleine Phillips (8)	50
Aaron Davies (7)	51
Carrie Lloyd (8)	52
Sean MacDonald (7)	53
Amy Roach (8)	54
Edward Evans (7)	55
Christian Ball (7)	56
Hannah Jones (8)	57
Kate Davies (8)	58
Harry Newman (8)	59
Kirsty Walsh (8)	60
Toby Mitten (7)	61
Emilie Gwilt (8)	62
Elizabeth Crosskey (7)	63
Nathan Sinclair (8)	64
Amy Barber-Brown (9)	65
Hayley Pugh (8)	66
Nikkita Jones (9)	67

Llanybydder Primary School, Llanybydder

Nadine Roderick (10)	68
Wyn Davies (10)	69
Sian Elin Williams (10)	70

Gemma Williams (11)   71
Toni Harding (11)   72

Sageston CP School, Sageston

Morgan Benbow (7)   73
Ben Brickle (7)   74
Charles Morgan (7)   75
Ben Andrews (8)   76
Shane Edwards (8)   77
Kurt Liddle (7)   78
James Taylor (8)   79
Louis Weston (8)   80
Carys Bates (7)   81
Odette Boyes (7)   82
Amy Compton (7)   83
Chloe Impey (7)   84
Holly Griffiths (8)   85
Stella Morgan (8)   86
Naomi Price (8)   87
Amy Ralph (7)   88
Sharmaine Richards (8)   89
Ebony Lindsay (10)   90
Shaun Whitfield (10)   91
Sophie Lovatt (10)   92
Daniel Bosley (9)   93
George Wilkins (10)   94
Samara Hicks (9)   95
Jake Mahoney (10)   96
Lydia Joyce (10)   97
Bridey Morgan (10)   98
Andrew Barnard (10)   99
Jacqs Scourfield (10)   100
Jools Parker (10)   101
Nicole Bevans (9)   102
Norton Williams (10)   103
Emma Thomas (10)   104
Lewis Brickle (10)   105
Marcus Read (10)   106

Ysgol Bethel, Caernarfon

Mari Pierce (9)	107
Caryl Slater-Parry (9)	108
Rebecca Jones (8)	109
Glesni Parry (9)	110
Wiliam Coles (9)	111
Eiry Price (9)	112
Elliott Duggan-Edwards (10)	113
Phoebe Lloyd-Hunter (10)	114
Poppy Holland-Williams (9)	115
Lois Jones (9)	116
Dylan Marc Hughes (9)	117
Ilid Jones (11)	118
Anna Wyn Jones (11)	119
Laura Owen (10)	120
Laura Jones (10)	121
Claudia Roberts (10)	122
Guto Griffiths (9)	123

Ysgol Bryncrug, Tywyn

Natalie Thomas (8)	124
Kayleigh Thomas (11)	125
Sophie Unsworth (10)	126
Iwan Jones (10)	127
Ava MacPherson (10)	128
Alicia Crane (9)	129
Thomas Davies (11)	130

Ysgol Cwm Y Glo, Caernarfon

Owen Cain (11)	131
Hannah Wilson (10)	132
Emma Smith (10)	133
Osian Davies (10)	134
Katie Roberts (10)	135
Dylan Jones (10)	136
Natasha Lowe-Sellers (11)	137
Conor Handy (10)	138
Patrick Griffith (10)	139
Jordan Lewis (11)	140
Aidan Christy (10)	141

The Poems

Spring!

Spring is not just another season,
Listen I have a reason,
After my poem you'll like spring too,
From buds on the trees to the morning dew,
Read my poem and you'll see just how wonderful
    Spring can be.

Spring is a time where plants grow,
It starts getting warmer, goodbye snow,
At spring leaves grow on trees,
Animals in fields, honey for bees,
Baby animals will be born,
All of which are adorn,
It can be cold, it can be hot,
But snow and storm are forgot,
This season brings festive fun,
It's enjoyed by everyone.
I hope you enjoyed my poem today,
Of a season called spring.
    March, April and May.

Matthew Antoniazzi (11)
Aberbargoed Primary School, Bargoed

Bonfire Night

B lazing fire in the night
O n the dew grass that shines so bright
N obody listens with care
F ireworks high in the air
I n the night the rockets shoot
R eally we're having a hoot
E verybody stops to look

N o one looks in the instruction book
I n the air fireworks go higher
G uy Fawkes burns on the fire
H ot dogs waiting on the stand
T he sparklers sparkle in your hand.

Megan Dunstone (11)
Aberbargoed Primary School, Bargoed

Poetry Day

It's poetry day but don't be sad,
'Cause poems are great and I am glad,
Poems are funny, short or long,
It may be a rhyme, but it's not a song.

So pick up a poem and have a look,
Poems are everywhere, just choose a book,
Read by yourself, or with a friend,
Start at the beginning and read to the end.

Poems offer so much so don't be a fool,
They're great, they're fun, they are really cool,
So I have wrote one more poem I hope you like it
After this one I promise I will sit . . .

P is for poems, it's poetry day
O is for outspoken, I'm sorry I have lots to say
E is for enjoy, read on your own or with friends
M is for many, many poems that never ever have to end.

Jodie Lehaj (11)
Aberbargoed Primary School, Bargoed

Spring Is . . .

Animals from their hibernation
The wind only a breeze
Birds all in their nests
Vegetables such as peas.

Lambs frolicking in the fields
New leaves on the trees
Rabbits hopping in their homes
And honey from the bees.

No more snow, grass on the earth
The sun has finally come out
The sheep have given birth.

Easter eggs because . . .
Easter's coming soon
The day has come and gone because . . .
It's night now not noon.

That's what spring is.

Lewis Gallent (10)
Aberbargoed Primary School, Bargoed

Guy Fawkes' Day

G oing to a firework display
U ntil the fire dies away
Y ou will come to this place with me

F or you will really like what you see
A mazing sights
W on't give you a fright
K ing of England nearly died
E verybody would have cried
S parklers sparkle in the dark

D oing pictures that leave a mark
A ll together everyone
Y ou can come and join the fun.

Jessica Lewis (11)
Aberbargoed Primary School, Bargoed

Winter Poem

W is for white snow
I is for the icicle dripping off the drain
N is for the nightmare which always comes at Christmas
T is for the tinsel to decorate the tree
E is for the elves helping Santa
R is for the reindeer pulling the sleigh
　　And that spells *winter*.

Rhys Pask (11)
Aberbargoed Primary School, Bargoed

Butterfly In The Sky

Butterfly in the sky
Quickly flying by
As I look I sigh
Something pretty
Has caught my eye.

Emma Halvey (11)
Aberbargoed Primary School, Bargoed

Springtime

Springtime is full of fun,
It is fun for everyone.
White sheep running around,
Rabbits hopping off the ground.
Birds tweeting in the trees,
Busy making honey are the bumblebees.
But outside it's still cold,
It's getting warmer I've been told.

Aidan Dauncey (11)
Aberbargoed Primary School, Bargoed

Fireworks

F lame slowly goes up the fuse
I nterstellar in the night
R eality seems like a dream
E mbers falling from the sky
W onders to the eye
O ver the moon
R ound and round
K ites seem low
S ing a song for the fireworks have come.

Aled Davies (11)
Aberbargoed Primary School, Bargoed

Winter

W is for winter when snow comes down
I is for ice that falls on the ground
N is for a never having a boring toy
T is for tinsel that goes around the tree
E is for elf that helps Santa
R is for Rudolph, he's got a red nose.

Hannah White (11)
Aberbargoed Primary School, Bargoed

Winter Poem

W inter is wet and windy
 I cicles dripping and melting
N ight lights are on, shadows going by
T insel shining on the tree at night
E lves are helping Santa
R udolph's nose shining bright.

Kieran Thomas (11)
Aberbargoed Primary School, Bargoed

Spring

In spring it is colourful
It is beautiful
It is wonderful
And in spring it is nice
Where the cats don't eat the mice
My cat sleeps in every day
The only time he gets up is when food is on its way.

Ashley Jones (10)
Aberbargoed Primary School, Bargoed

Winter

W inter time is full of joy
I t is fun for each girl and boy
N uts are brought out on Christmas Day
T insel is put around the bay
E xcited children sing one song
R eindeers gallop all night long.

Josh Adams (11)
Aberbargoed Primary School, Bargoed

Bonfire

B ang in the air the firework has gone off
O is for orange sparklers in your hand
N is for night the fireworks go off
F is for a fire with Guy Fawkes on top
 I is for in the sky the fireworks go off
R is for a rocket that goes bang in the air
E is for the end we have to leave
     So see you later when fireworks go.

Anna Jeffery (11)
Aberbargoed Primary School, Bargoed

Winter

Falling from the sky white bitter snow fell
Still all night quietly grew colder
Suddenly the snow turned grey and wet.

Anthony Lewis (11)
Aberbargoed Primary School, Bargoed

Hate

Hate sounds like rocks smashing on the ground.
Hate looks like lightning falling down.
Hate tastes like hot sauce burning in your mouth.
Hate smells like fire sparkling in the south.

Lewis Williams (11)
Carreghofa Primary School, Llanymynech

Emotions

Love is the colour of pink like a booming heart.
Fear is the taste of hot fiery curry.
Fun is the sound of party poppers popping everywhere.
Anger looks like the spicy red eyes of a devil.
Happiness reminds me of the birds in a tree singing.
Hate smells like burnt chips in a frying pan.

Clare Sides (10)
Carreghofa Primary School, Llanymynech

Anger

Anger sounds like the Devil making madness.
It tastes like thunder crackling in my mouth.
Anger smells like smoke in the air.
It looks like forty days with no food.
Anger reminds us of death on stormy nights.

Rachel Arthur & Vicky Roberts (8)
Carreghofa Primary School, Llanymynech

Excitement

Excitement is orange
Like a kite playing in the wind
Excitement tastes like your heart is in your throat
Excitement feels like a cool ice cream dipped in melted chocolate
Dripping on my tongue
Excitement looks like a cat about to pounce on a mouse.

Chelsea Lloyd & Yasmin Wydell (10)
Carreghofa Primary School, Llanymynech

Emotions And Feelings

Hunger feels like a volcano about to erupt.
Sadness tastes like an onion being cut.
Silence sounds like the calm waters of the sea.
Hate smells like the hot smoky fumes coming from the bonfire.
Love looks like the melting chocolate of Lindor trickling down
                                                    your throat.
Anger tastes like a hot Vindaloo sitting on your tongue.
Fun sounds like children playing at the fair.
Laughter feels like a bumpy roller coaster going round and round
                                        and up and down.
Nervousness looks like a jelly wobbling on a plate.

Paige Lloyd & Chloe James (11)
Carreghofa Primary School, Llanymynech

My Special Place

Down the grassy, sandy track,
Onto the picturesque beach,
I quickly ran to my special place,
That I keep for only me.

I climbed up the rugged, rocky face,
To my special seat on the cliff,
I sat and admired the rolling waves,
That gently washed the sand with their frothy white foam.

I sat there motionless, gazing ahead,
The birds that hover on the horizon,
Ships sailed into the bay,
I could see them from my special place.

There I sat upon the dark, black cliff,
Watching the sun go slowly down
The sky turned a pinky-orange,
I was left on the beach alone.

Shona Hughes (10)
Cradoc School, Brecon

A Bird Of Prey

The huge bird flew over
Wings spread in the air
Talons outstretched
Waiting for its prey
Diving down like a bullet
The huge bird with its prey.

Luke Bowen
Cradoc School, Brecon

The Mysterious Stone

The stone was dull as sky,
The colours were dark as could be,
There were blues, pinks and greens,
Then the magnificent colours came to life,
And the stone stood still.

Rough like a tree trunk,
Smooth as soft silk,
Sharp as splinters of glass,
Bumpy as rippled sand,
And the stone stood still.

Wet like the crashing waves,
Cracked as an old person's skin,
Lumpy as cold custard,
Swirly colours everywhere,
And the stone stood still.

Hannah Cowley (11)
Cradoc School, Brecon

The Great Lion

Eats meat as if it's really soft
Its teeth are as sharp as a shark's
Claws like a knife
The same as a cat but more deadly
It's as warm as the sun
So watch out, it's the lion.

Rhys Morris (7)
Guilsfield CP School, Welshpool

The Red Kite

Flying against the breeze
Chestnul coal
Against a turquoise sky
Swooping to grab a startled mouse
Below the wild Welsh mountains
With its sharp and terrible talons
And horrendously hooked beak
Tearing the meat apart
Before soaring beautifully
Its forked tail like a rudder
High above mid Wales.

Megan Davies (7)
Guilsfield CP School, Welshpool

Red Kite

Talons as strong as iron
Beak curled like a fishing hook
If you see a chestnut dot
Plunging down into the ground
Protect it
It's a red kite.

Lewis Williams (7)
Guilsfield CP School, Welshpool

Sports Day

Running, running,
All around parents cheering
On the ground, children racing
Like a hare looking like they
Just don't care.

I'm in my sack ready
To race and hopefully
I'll win first place,
It does not matter where you
Come at least you're all
Having fun!

Alex Cawthra (9)
Guilsfield CP School, Welshpool

Cats

I heard a little cat,
Creeping on the mat,
He tried to steal the food,
As he was in a good mood,
The cat had a nap
On my grandad's cap.

He likes to climb trees
He does this
With ease at night
He sits by the fire
On top of the big black tyre.

Michael Jones (8)
Guilsfield CP School, Welshpool

Imagination

What do you call an imagination?
A daydream of life sleeping or awake,
Leaping and jumping,
No matter where you are,
You will always have your imagination.

Jack Windsor (9)
Guilsfield CP School, Welshpool

My Horse

My horse is jumping
My horse is cantering
My horse's mane blows in the breeze
His long legs buck high in the air
I can hear them running up and down on the steep hill
They are coming.

Stephanie Lloyd (9)
Guilsfield CP School, Welshpool

Football

Football is fun,
Just like eating a bun.
The aim is to score a goal,
Just like Ashley Cole.
Screaming fans at the game,
Just like famous football players.

Kieran Done (9)
Guilsfield CP School, Welshpool

George The Saviour

I'll tell a story of a fortunate village that was saved by George himself.
In a village far away,
People heard a mighty roar but kept on drinking beer!
Smashing mountains, clawing houses, firing fire in the land.
'Flee, flee for your life,
I'm afraid the dragon is here!
Gather the army, attack, attack!'
So they made arrangements here, there to take him on,
But alas that did not work.
'George, George, call George,
We're under attack from a mighty plague!'
Swish, swish goes his sword, hooray the dragon is gone,
So that is the tale,
Bye-bye be gone!

Billy Pringle (9)
Guilsfield CP School, Welshpool

Cars

Cars really, really fast
As they go zooming
Revving engines at the start
Waiting on the grid for green to depart
Ramming into walls
Wheels spinning like footballs
Coming in 1st place
People hoping they win the race.

Andrew Davies (9)
Guilsfield CP School, Welshpool

On The Playground

Children running all around
Some falling on the ground
Some playing the game Bloodhounds
Some wearing bright red gowns.
Five playing hide-and-seek
With one answering with cheek.
Three avoiding the teacher's look
They can't wait till they read a book.
Two playing in a row
One, two, three and off we go
Some staying very low,
Stopping themselves to go!

Oliver Hart (9)
Guilsfield CP School, Welshpool

Power Rangers

They protect the world from evil,
With the help of their Zords,
They fight with feet and hands,
They will defeat Master Org,
Red, yellow, white, silver and black,
These are the colours that will help attack,
Winning fights is what they do,
To scare the baddies they shout *boo!*
While doing front flips in the air,
Always watching in their lair.

Garion Brown (9)
Guilsfield CP School, Welshpool

Racing Cars

Racing at the speed of light,
People cheering for every car.
Tarmac steaming with wheels speeding.
The crowds shouting at them to win.
Winning trophies gleaming in the sun.
Everyone crosses the line,
Squeaking across the line,
But they were moving fine!

Cameron Davies (9)
Guilsfield CP School, Welshpool

My Dog

My dog is Brandy
She likes to play with her toys
She is very cute.

My dog is Brandy
She is only twelve months old
I love her so much.

My dog is Brandy
She jumps up at me
And then she licks me.

My dog is Brandy
Someone needs to play with her
She is my best friend.

Mollie Allen (9)
Guilsfield CP School, Welshpool

My Cats Tabby And Ginger

My cats are Tabby and Ginger
The fat one eats while the skinny one drinks
When I sit by the fire
They both sit on my lap
They're so soft I start to sneeze
They are so fast
They would win a place in the marathon.

Charlotte Pearce (9)
Guilsfield CP School, Welshpool

Recipe For A Pet Rabbit

First wash your hands as clean as a whistle
Next get a bowl as big as a magician's hat
Then put in a brush with soft white bristles
Mix in some whiskers from the cat.
Sprinkle in some chocolate for his button nose
Two fresh leeks for his ears, long and flopping
Add a handful of stars for his twinkle toes
Two bright diamond eyes to see where he's hopping.

Ryan Jones (9)
Guilsfield CP School, Welshpool

Charlie Brown

Charlie Brown, my special dog
Sometimes snorted like a hog.
A Basset hound
I'd never have put in the pound.
We played together from dusk to dawn,
Playing together on the lawn.
Then the day came when he passed away,
My only dog saying hip hip hooray!
A heart attack is how he died,
All the time I cried,
That dog I loved him,
That dog I miss him,
That dog Charlie Brown.

Mary-Morgan Griffiths (9)
Guilsfield CP School, Welshpool

The Playground

People crying
People running
Children singing a happy song
Dogs yapping
Birds flapping
Children having a snooze
Children clapping
People snapping
Everybody's having a good day.

Lauren Jones (9)
Guilsfield CP School, Welshpool

I Am Rushing To School

I am rushing to school
Mum saying, 'Come on, come on.'
I am hurrying to school
Mum saying, 'Come on, come on.'
Baby brother in his buggy
Crying for his dummy
We all jump in the car
Mum saying, 'Hurry up, hurry up!'
'Where's my lunch box?'
'On the bar!'
Mum saying, 'You're late, you're late.'
No friends waiting at the gate
Mum saying, 'You're late, you're late.'
Along the path Mum saying, 'You're late, you're late.'
When I get there, oh no! It's Saturday!

Melanie Humphreys (8)
Guilsfield CP School, Welshpool

The Judo Poem

Judo, judo is so wonderful,
Jump on the mat and ray.
Running round the mat until
You're ready to fight.

Imagine winning a medal,
(Gold that's right).
Using your energy with all your might.
To win that gold,
So you feel bold,
Going home is a sad thing
Because you can't fight,
Right!

Alisha Bourne (8)
Guilsfield CP School, Welshpool

The Graceful Swan

I saw a very special swan
It was eating the fish in the pond
Its eyes were like streams
And its feathers were like white beams
Then it gracefully swam out of the pond
It started running for a very smooth take-off
Then gliding, soaring, flying
So now
Look out for the graceful swan
It might be nesting in your pond.

Sarah Williams (7)
Guilsfield CP School, Welshpool

The Graceful Cat

At the black of night the graceful cat
Comes with eyes like two sparkling disco balls
And fur the colour of the golden eagle
Creeping as silent as a mouse
Darting through the dewy grasslands
As elegantly as a red kite
Unsuspected victim, run
Because you're being hunted -
So just beware
The cat's about.

Aaron Williams (7)
Guilsfield CP School, Welshpool

My Red Kite

A beautiful morning
The sky is light as gold
As I watch my special kite
It's not a bird to hover
With its talons
As sharp as sharks' teeth
It shoots down like lightning
Air breather
A red kite racing
Across the wind in Wales.

Rhys Sinnett
Guilsfield CP School, Welshpool

My Labrador

Cat slayer
Shoe chewer
Bowl licker
Ball player
Tail wagger
Sleep maker
Postman biter.

Seren Childs (8)
Guilsfield CP School, Welshpool

The Marvellous Bird

As fast as a lightning bolt
To take you by surprise
A robber of carrion
A beak as sharp as the sharpest knife
So very hazardous to a mouse
Swooping down like red lightning
With talons penetrating the quivering body.

James Gretton (8)
Guilsfield CP School, Welshpool

My Cat Ginger

Eyes bright like crystals
Fur soft like a teddy bear
Tail long, twitching
Like a lion's -
My beautiful ginger
Mouse eater.

Amie Baines (7)
Guilsfield CP School, Welshpool

Red Kite

A red kite racing the wind
And darting through misty clouds.
The fork-tailed eagle, king of the sky
He soars and glides on the breeze.
The conker-coloured bird,
With the most amazing wings
That float in the air as he soars against the wind.
His call is as loud as a drum
And his talons pierce his prey,
The mouse.
'Oh what a beautiful bird!'

Madeleine Phillips (8)
Guilsfield CP School, Welshpool

Red Kite

Red kite
Faster than any bird in the sky
Faster than a cheetah
Reddish-brown bird colour
Protected by the people
Not like the olden days
The kite's soul
Blown by the wind
Chestnut belly
Above its prey
On the land
Grabbing a mouse
Or rubbish
In its talons
It lives here in Wales
But it nearly didn't
What a beautiful bird
Black wings
Big strong beak
My favourite bird.

Aaron Davies (7)
Guilsfield CP School, Welshpool

The Graceful Swan

Clear deep pool
Fringed with bulrushes
With the sticky mud
Glistening in the rain
When the rain stops
We see the shining dew
And then the swan
Coming out of the bulrushes
Watch it gliding
The queen of this royal pool
Wings held high
An invisible crown
Balanced on a snow-white
Feathered head.

Carrie Lloyd (8)
Guilsfield CP School, Welshpool

Wonderless Bluebells

Beautiful coloured petals
Wild wonderful dancing leaves
Delicate nodding flowers
Like bells, only blue
A soft breeze blows them around
And I can almost hear them.

Sean MacDonald (7)
Guilsfield CP School, Welshpool

Red Bird

Amazing fork-tailed bird
Soaring through the sky like red lightning
Swooping down to catch its prey
Gliding through the valleys
Among the wild green mountains.

Amy Roach (8)
Guilsfield CP School, Welshpool

My Sheepdog

Sheep herder
Bone muncher
Cat chaser
Van-ride hitcher
Loud barker
Wheel attacker
Fast runner.

Edward Evans (7)
Guilsfield CP School, Welshpool

My Corn Snake

Wrist strangler
Skin shedder
Mouse biter
Tongue flicker
Whole prey swallower
Chloe
My slithering fork-tongued
Corn snake.

Christian Ball (7)
Guilsfield CP School, Welshpool

Creeping Crawler

Caterpillars are amazing creatures
If they fill up on leaves
They will outgrow their skin
And transform into a lifeless-looking chrysalis
But hidden inside is . . .
A delicate butterfly
Waiting, painted in lovely colours
To flutter about all day long.

Hannah Jones (8)
Guilsfield CP School, Welshpool

Amazing Red Kite

A red kite
Gliding in the summer breeze
Swooping down the valley
Its sharp knife-edge beak
And talons to catch its prey
Down in the valley
Before escaping with it to its nest.

Kate Davies (8)
Guilsfield CP School, Welshpool

The Horse

Lane trotter
Hoof glider
Hand licker
Hedge jumper
Fast shooter
Tail swisher.

Harry Newman (8)
Guilsfield CP School, Welshpool

Pets

My pets are two cats and two rabbits,
I could have different animals but I'm not allowed!
I feel the fur of my very soft cat
As I go to put on my very best hat,
I play hide-and-seek with the rabbits,
This has become a bit of a habit,
I know one day they will leave my side,
I will then have to run and hide.

Kirsty Walsh (8)
Guilsfield CP School, Welshpool

King Cobra

In the lightness
Hissing at the air -
The people said,
'It's a snake, beware.'
One person threw in a mouse
The snake ate it
As if it were eating a chip
The king cobra
Shed its skin
As easily
As peeling a banana.

Toby Mitten (7)
Guilsfield CP School, Welshpool

Red Kite

Like lightning when it swoops
Down for its prey
Fishing for carrion
With its sharp hooked beak
It lives in mid Wales
On wild mountains
A forked tail steers
The red kite
In the sapphire sky.

Emilie Gwilt (8)
Guilsfield CP School, Welshpool

Midnight

A fox's tail is fluffy like a ball of wool.
Eyes as black as rain clouds in the howling sky.
Ears as orange as fire
On a bonfire burning.
Bones as strong as iron.
Blood as hot as the sun booming out of the sky
Danger's on its way
The hounds and hunters
Are on their way.

Elizabeth Crosskey (7)
Guilsfield CP School, Welshpool

The Snake That Had A Baby In School

I was excited
But a bit nervous -
A snake in school
Christian's corn snake
When I held it
Something was coming out of its tail.
It was a baby, a tiny snake.
I called Christian
Told him what happened
And he told his dad.

Nathan Sinclair (8)
Guilsfield CP School, Welshpool

Life In My Bungalow

Last night in my bungalow nothing was stirring below,
In the bungalow me, Mum and Ces were sitting in the living room
About to have a rest,
We were about to watch a movie.
I was hoping to watch something groovy,
But instead it was something pretty scary.
Halfway through the movie,
Though we have no neighbours,
Sometimes I have to do Ces some favours.
The movie's over, I go to bed feeling scared,
I think I am going to have a . . .
Nightmare!

Amy Barber-Brown (9)
Guilsfield CP School, Welshpool

Teachers

Teachers are kind when they sound cheerful
Teachers help us and take us on trips on the bus.
Teachers get stuck when I bring in a rubber duck
Teachers nag when kids forget their bag
Teachers teach languages when eating their sandwiches
Teachers need to work out because they can't count.

Hayley Pugh (8)
Guilsfield CP School, Welshpool

School

Some subjects in school can be very cool
There's sports and science and art
Some subjects they can be boring but fair
Come what may it's a 9am start.

Nikkita Jones (9)
Guilsfield CP School, Welshpool

Family And Friends

I have a friend called Kayleigh
She likes to annoy me.
I also have a friend called Natalie
She likes to play tricks on me.
All my friends are special to me
I hope they don't forget me.

My family are very special to me
They are protective of me.
They play with me most of the time
In the summer we have barbecues all the time.

Back to my friends again,
I have four extra friends Sian Elin, Lauren, Alice and Toni.
They are my best friends so they are very special to me.

I have lots of family
They make me laugh and sometimes make me cry.
They are the best family I could ask for.
I don't get to see them all every day, but they are still there with me.

Nadine Roderick (10)
Llanybydder Primary School, Llanybydder

Quad Biking

Quad biking is my sport
We do it all the time.
It never gets old because it's vroom vroom time
I've done it all my lifetime
And water goes through my pipeline
To run my quad all day.

I'll never give it up
Because it's my thing.
I come third all the time
Because it's my thing.

Wyn Davies (10)
Llanybydder Primary School, Llanybydder

Holiday

Bright sun shimmers
On holiday
The glistening
Water that
Sparkles
When the sun
Is shining.

Fun and laughter
Water and sun
If you put
Them together
You have a
Brilliant time.

Fantastic friends
A cool
Disco
Wicked
Entertainment
What a lovely
Holiday.

Sian Elin Williams (10)
Llanybydder Primary School, Llanybydder

Sweets And Sweets

Sweets and sweets with cherry tops
Where you get them shops and shops.
Flavoured lollies and fizzy drinks
When you get there you're sure to faint.
Children's dreams are in the shop
What else would you want?
The man is friendly.
The house is made out of candy!
What a shock!
      Here we go!

Gemma Williams (11)
Llanybydder Primary School, Llanybydder

The Old Ways

The old ways have been forgotten,
Stolen and lost.

They have taken lives and villages,
At a huge cost.

We tried to save them,
Even though it was hard,

With all our might
As thick as lard.

One day they'll come,
Astray back to me.

I'll try to remain,
Traditional as can be.

Toni Harding (11)
Llanybydder Primary School, Llanybydder

The Child Of The Year

January's child is very funny.
February's child is like a bunny.
March's child likes chewing gum.
April's child likes writing sums.
May's child likes breaking toys.
June's child makes all the noise.
July's child is like a dad.
August's child is sometimes mad!
September's child likes lots of honey.
October's child likes lots of money.
November's child is very bold.
December's child is sometimes cold.

Morgan Benbow (7)
Sageston CP School, Sageston

The Child Of The Year

January's child is very bad,
February's child is sometimes sad.
March's child loves to kick and scream.
April's child is in a dream.
May's child is very funny,
June's child likes money.
July's child likes to run.
August's child lies in the sun.
September's child always gets stung.
October's child is very young.
November's child is very bold.
December's child has a streaming cold.

Ben Brickle (7)
Sageston CP School, Sageston

The Child Of The Year

January's child is sad and mad,
February's child is mad and bad.
March's child is very young,
April's child is always stung.
May's child is sunny and funny,
June's child is very funny.
July's child is very glad,
August's child has got a dad.
September's child likes to sleep,
October's child likes to leap.
November's child is so gay,
December's child likes to play.

Charles Morgan (7)
Sageston CP School, Sageston

The Child Of The Week

Monday's child is like a monkey,
Tuesday's child wears clothes so chunky.
Wednesday's child likes to have fun,
Thursday's child goes for a run.
Friday's child throws a fit,
Saturday's child likes to sit.
The child that is born on the seventh day,
Is funny and nice and happy all day.

Ben Andrews (8)
Sageston CP School, Sageston

Child Of The Year

January's child is big and strong.
February's child is tall and long.
March's child likes to eat honey.
April's child is a bit funny.
May's child is a lot sweet.
June's child is very neat.
July's child is very fair.
August's child is always somewhere.
September's child is very good.
October's child is not so good.
November's child is full of grace.
December's child is going to space.

Shane Edwards (8)
Sageston CP School, Sageston

The Child Of The Week

Monday's child is funny and loves honey.
Tuesday's child is sunny and loves money.
Wednesday's child is getting mad.
Thursday's child is very bad.
Friday's child has found a shell.
Saturday's child fell in a well.
And the child that is born on the seventh day
Is very sensible.

Kurt Liddle (7)
Sageston CP School, Sageston

The Child Of The Year

January's child is bad and mad
February's child is sad glad
March's child is cold and funny
April's child is extremely sunny.
May's child is sleepy and weepy
June's child is sneaky and leapy.
July's child is kind of sad
August's child will be a good dad.
September's child will be a bit bolder
October's child will be a year older.
November's child is never bad
December's child will be a good lad.

James Taylor (8)
Sageston CP School, Sageston

Child Of The Week

Monday's child is full of fun,
Tuesday's child is full of sun.
Wednesday's child fell in a sleep,
Thursday's child fell in a heap!
Friday's child went to the beach,
Saturday's child ate a soft peach.
The child that is born on the seventh day
Is happy and glad and good all day.

Louis Weston (8)
Sageston CP School, Sageston

The Child Of The Year

January's child is very bad,
February's child is very sad.
March's child is mad and funny,
April's child likes all the money.
May's child is tall and thin,
June's child tries hard to win.
July's child likes the wild,
August's child is very mild.
September's child is sunny and fair,
October's child is like a mare.
November's child is fair and clear,
December's child has got a lot of fear.

Carys Bates (7)
Sageston CP School, Sageston

The Child Of The Week

Monday's child is very sad,
Tuesday's child is very mad.
Wednesday's child is big and fat,
Thursday's child is like a bat,
Friday's child is like a cat,
Saturday's child is full of honey,
Sunday's child is very funny.

Odette Boyes (7)
Sageston CP School, Sageston

The Child Of The Week

Monday's child is really funny.
Tuesday's child has a lot of money.
Wednesday's child is getting mad.
Thursday's child is getting bad.
Friday's child is getting fat.
Saturday's child has a bat.
The child who is born on the seventh day
Is nice and kind and sensible, OK.

Amy Compton (7)
Sageston CP School, Sageston

The Child Of The Week

Monday's child is pink and funny
Tuesday's child is yellow and sunny.
Wednesday's child is gold and likes honey
Thursday's child is green and likes money.
Friday's child is blue and cold
Saturday's child is black and bold.
The child that is born on the seventh day
Is happy and glad like a rainbow in May.

Chloe Impey (7)
Sageston CP School, Sageston

The Child Of The Year

January's child is young and small,
February's child is old and tall.
March's child is bad and sad,
April's child is mad and glad.
May's child is full of fun,
June's child likes to run.
July's child likes to jump,
August's child had a bump.
September's child had a ball,
October's child had a call.
November's child is good and funny,
December's child likes his money.

Holly Griffiths (8)
Sageston CP School, Sageston

The Child Of The Year

January's child is very bad,
February's child is always mad,
March's child is chilled and cool,
April's child is a big, big fool,
May's child has just got stung,
June's child is very young,
July's child likes a lot of honey,
August's child is never funny,
September's child is very strong,
October's child is never wrong,
November's child is good at maths,
December's child has a lot of baths!

Stella Morgan (8)
Sageston CP School, Sageston

The Child Of The Week

Monday's child is smart and funny,
Tuesday's child like sunny honey.
Wednesday's child is mad and glad,
Thursday's child is sad and bad.
Friday's child is hunky and chunky,
Saturday's child jumps like a monkey.
The child that is born on the seventh day
Is good and kind and works all day.

Naomi Price (8)
Sageston CP School, Sageston

The Child Of The Week

Monday's child is full of joy
Tuesday's child is a handsome boy
Wednesday's child is full of fun
Thursday's child is in the sun.
Friday's child has some money
Saturday's child likes runny honey.
The child that is born on the seventh day
Is a clever boy, 'Hip hip hooray!'

Amy Ralph (7)
Sageston CP School, Sageston

The Child Of The Year

January's child is very, very funny.
February's child likes eating honey.
March's child is glad he has a dad.
April's child is a really bad lad.
May's child makes all the noise.
June's child has all the toys.
July's child has a dance.
August's child has a prance.
September's child flings his books.
October's child has extremely nice looks.
November's child is very, very tall,
December's child is sweet and small.

Sharmaine Richards (8)
Sageston CP School, Sageston

Mary Poppins Where Are You?

Mary Poppins where are you?
I need to tidy my room
I need to use the polish, mop and broom.
I started it this morning
And my mum will be up soon
Have you seen the time already it's the middle of the afternoon.
Mary Poppins where are you?

Ebony Lindsay (10)
Sageston CP School, Sageston

Germany 2006

G reat things will be happening
E ngland will be there
R onaldo, Ronaldinho - Brazilians with flare!
M unich, Berlin with great stadiums to play
A rmies of supporters arriving every day
N inth of July, the winner we will see
Y es, be warned, football's on TV!

Shaun Whitfield (10)
Sageston CP School, Sageston

The Beach

When we are on the beach we have so much fun.
When we are lying in the sun.
All the children have buckets and spades.
Some enjoy swimming in the waves.

Sophie Lovatt (10)
Sageston CP School, Sageston

Where Do The Cows Go?

Please Mr Farmer where do all the cows go?
It's a quarter past three, are they going in for tea?
The farmer looked at me and said,
In a voice soft and slow,
'Milking is where they are off to go!'
So that is where all the cows go,
At a quarter past three.

Daniel Bosley (9)
Sageston CP School, Sageston

Everton

Everton is my team
Nickname is the blues,
I love it when we win
But am sad when we lose.
Tim Cahill is the best
And I like David Moyes,
When they play I like to shout,
'Come on you blue boys!'

George Wilkins (10)
Sageston CP School, Sageston

Eyes

Eyes are big,
Eyes are round,
Eyes are far up from
The ground.

Eyes are brown,
Eyes are blue,
I have eyes and so do you.

Samara Hicks (9)
Sageston CP School, Sageston

I Thought I'd Done It All

I had a dream, I scored a goal
I really thought I'd done it all
The crowd did scream, rant and rave
They did the Mexican wave.
My teammates couldn't believe their eyes,
It really was a big surprise.
The ball went in from the centre half
I couldn't believe it was a laugh.
I was so chuffed I'd scored a goal
I'm really gonna keep that ball.
I'll place it in a special box
Right next to my lucky socks.

Jake Mahoney (10)
Sageston CP School, Sageston

Pembrokeshire

Sandy beaches
Windswept shores
Such a beautiful place
Who would want to stay indoors?

Magical castles
Fields full of daffodils
And boats on shiny waters
With bright and colourful sails.

I'm glad I live in Pembrokeshire
I couldn't live elsewhere
For home is where the heart is
And mine is right here.

Lydia Joyce (10)
Sageston CP School, Sageston

Big Sisters

Big sisters get on my wick
When I go shopping they don't know what to pick!
They fall in love with the most ugly guys!
And I really have to ask myself why?
They stay up late and watch TV
When they walk in to annoy and laugh
I have to shout *leave me be!*

Bridey Morgan (10)
Sageston CP School, Sageston

At The Swing Of A Bat

The cricket season has begun
My cricket ball just swung
The ball cracks against my bat
How's that! The umpire shouts, 'You're out!'

Oh no! Out for a duck
Where is my luck?
I storm from the crease
When will this misery cease?

Bowling now, my chance has come
I'll show them how
My spin will spring
Up to the batter's shoulder.

Past his head, the ball spins by
Whistles past his earhole
He dodges it, whoa take it easy
He's looking kinda queasy.

Wicket keeper's on the ground
He's hunched up in a ball
What's up with him?
It seems he's been taken with a googlie.

Well that's that
The batter's sick
And the wickie needs first aid
And all at the swing of a bat.

Andrew Barnard (10)
Sageston CP School, Sageston

School

I can smell hard work all around,
In the classrooms brains pound,
I can hear the sound of clocks ticking,
Soon be playtime - balls kicking
I can taste the cook's latest concoction
Healthy dinners now - chips not an option
I can see the mums arrive
Home time soon, tea at five.

Jacqs Scourfield (10)
Sageston CP School, Sageston

Train Journey

Out of the station the carriage pushes,
Over the hill and past the bushes.
Faster and faster through the day,
All the children start to play.

A sheep in the field starts to baa,
Then the rest start right there.
A cow in the paddock starts to moo,
Then the rest do it too.

A horse in the field starts to neigh,
Then another sits on hay.
A man in a car beeps his horn,
While his son is eating corn.

Into the station the carriage pushes,
Down the hill and past the bushes.
Slower and slower goes the train,
Then we get home again.

Jools Parker (10)
Sageston CP School, Sageston

Mexico, Mexico

Mexico, Mexico,
So up high,
Mexico, Mexico,
In the sky,
Mexico, Mexico,
So low down,
Mexico, Mexico,
Where are you now?

Nicole Bevans (9)
Sageston CP School, Sageston

My Dad

I love my dad so much,
Even if he is Dutch.
He drives me in his car,
It's a TVR.
We go fast and slow,
My goodness that car can go.

Norton Williams (10)
Sageston CP School, Sageston

I Love To Do My Homework

I love to do my homework,
It makes me feel good.
I love to do exactly
As my teacher says I should.

I love to do my homework,
I never miss a day.
I even love the men in white
Who are taking me away.

Emma Thomas (10)
Sageston CP School, Sageston

Digging In The Garden

Digging in the garden what will we find?
A dinosaur all scaly and red,
Or even parts of an old-fashioned bed.
Pirates' treasure, silver and gold
Or even a coin from when the world was old.
Maybe old photos from when the Vikings were here,
Or for Dad, some old cans of beer.
World War weapons, guns and swords,
Or maybe old models of Fords.
Or just moles and rabbits, but mostly moles,
If you want to find out dig some holes.
What will we find?

Lewis Brickle (10)
Sageston CP School, Sageston

A Young Man From China

There was a young man from China
Who thought he would be a good miner
When he was told you go underground
He turned around and frowned
Which displeased that young man of China.

Marcus Read (10)
Sageston CP School, Sageston

The Sun

The sun is a twinkly,
Huge and hot fairy,
Who sits warm and comfy,
High up in the sky.

She has two shiny bright eyes,
And a lovely smile for a mouth.

She lives in the big bright blue sky,
With her friends,
The stars,
The moon,
And all others.

When the day has been
And the night has come,
The sun sleeps quietly on the moon.

When the sun is asleep
She dreams of
Shining brightly over the world.

The rain is her father
And the wind is her mother,
And one day the sun will burn the Earth.

Mari Pierce (9)
Ysgol Bethel, Caernarfon

Snowdon

Snowdon is a large, fluffy
And cuddly panda,
With giant blue eyes
And a mouthful of bamboo.
He has a tiny, slimy tongue,
And very white teeth.
He lives inside a mountain
And sleeps by a rock.
He dreams of eating day and night
And sometimes, even
Giving you a fright!
His parents are the sun and sky.

One day he will escape from
His dungeon-like home.

Caryl Slater-Parry (9)
Ysgol Bethel, Caernarfon

The Wind

The wind is a ghost,
He has two colossal blue and green eyes.
He eats old trees
And
Fresh new flowers
And roots for
Snacks.
He lives in the
Clouds up in the sky.
He sleeps on stars.
He dreams of
Blowing everybody away!
His dad is rain
His mam is the snow.
He will make the wind so strong
That he can open the door!

Rebecca Jones (8)
Ysgol Bethel, Caernarfon

The Sun

The sun is a huge
Fire-breathing dragon
With big round eyes.
He has a ginormous
Mouth like a big cave.
He lives up by
The stars in the sky.
Inside a beautiful mansion
On a hot, hot star.
He sleeps on a humungous
Rock just outside his house.
He dreams of burning
Everything on Earth.
His mum is the stars
And his father is the moon.
One day he will burn
The whole place down and
Rule the world.

Glesni Parry (9)
Ysgol Bethel, Caernarfon

The Storm

The storm is a huge, large,
Substantial eagle,
That plunges down to Earth
Like a comet.
The storm has ten
Considerable,
Mighty,
Evil,
Dark eyes that
Glow in the night.
His mouth is like a hulking rock
Floating in the air
It lives in a palace
Up in the clouds.
It sleeps in a dark
And damp dungeon.
It dreams of ruling the world.
His mother is the sun,
And his father is Snowdon.
And one day he will learn how to
Build houses back up again.

Wiliam Coles (9)
Ysgol Bethel, Caernarfon

The Rain

The rain is an insect
Falling from the sky.
She has eyes for stars.
She has a mouth hiding in the clouds.
She lives far away in the North Pole.
She sleeps in the
Deep blue sea.
She dreams of flooding the Earth.
Her dad is a tornado.
Her mother is a
Huge waterfall.
One day
She will gather her friends and family
And rule the Earth
With an evil smile.

Eiry Price (9)
Ysgol Bethel, Caernarfon

Happiness

Happiness is playing Nintendo DS on the last level of Super Mario.
It smells like a match day programme whilst I am reading it.
It tastes like a cheeseburger in McDonald's breaking in my mouth.
It sounds like the 3, 2, 1 on the Rock n Roller coaster in Disney
                                                    Studios.
It feels like being on the Rock 'n' Roller coaster in Disneyland.
It lives in the city of Manchester Stadium.
It is famous like Ronaldinho.
It supports Man City and it hates Man U and Chelsea.
Is watching Friends on E4 and E4+.

Elliott Duggan-Edwards (10)
Ysgol Bethel, Caernarfon

Love

Love is a red ruby shimmering in the shining sun.
It smells like roses and lilies swaying in the summer breeze.
It tastes like a giant marshmallow cookie,
Dipped in freshly melted chocolate.
It sounds like the sea lapping gently at the shore,
Washing over the rocks at the beautiful beach of Penmon.
It feels like my sumptuously, fluffy cat,
Purring melodiously at the end of my bed.
It lives in everybody, everywhere, rich and poor,
Black and white, young and old.

Most of the time!

Phoebe Lloyd-Hunter (10)
Ysgol Bethel, Caernarfon

Happiness

Happiness is like chocolate melting,
It smells like Cocoa beans in Cadburyland,
It tastes like ice cream sundae, melting in your mouth,
It sounds like crisps munching in your mouth,
It feels like soft silk on your quilt,
It lives in my house most of the time.

Poppy Holland-Williams (9)
Ysgol Bethel, Caernarfon

Happiness

Happiness is the flowers in the field singing on a sunny day.
It smells like the red poppy in my garden in front of my
                                    bedroom window.
It tastes like a giant chocolate chip cookie being baked
                                    by my grandma.
It sounds like the birds singing every morning at seven
                                    when I wake up.
It feels like the sun sparkling in your eyes.
It lives in my house most of the sunny time.

Lois Jones (9)
Ysgol Bethel, Caernarfon

Embarrassment

Embarrassment is an evil curse
Sent from the cruel devil.
It smells like
Burning fire
And people from the dead
Coming alive.
It tastes like all the smelly garbage
In the universe.
It sounds like the end of the world
And that you have stepped into another dimension.
It feels like the stinking detention.
It lives all around me.

Dylan Marc Hughes (9)
Ysgol Bethel, Caernarfon

Beauty

Beauty is a flower
That lives across the road
That desires my heart
And makes the sun last forever.

It smells like fresh home-made bread
That's ready to make lovely jam sandwiches
For tea tonight for all the family.

It tastes like choc chip mint ice cream
That's ready to be eaten before it will melt
With the roasting sun by the river.

It sounds like a blessing from God
It makes you feel happy and cheerful.

It feels like you could eat forever and ever
And makes you feel happy and blissful inside.

It lives in my heart
That bleeds with joy.

Ilid Jones (11)
Ysgol Bethel, Caernarfon

Ugliness

Ugliness is the ugly fat woman
In the horrible house next door.
It smells like a dustbin in the summer.
It tastes like stinking Brussels sprouts.
It sounds like frightening thunder
Ripping the black sky in two pieces.
It feels like disgusting rubbish.
It lives in the horrible house next door.

Anna Wyn Jones (11)
Ysgol Bethel, Caernarfon

Happiness

Happiness is melted chocolate flowing like a river.
It smells like lavender swaying softly in the wind.
It tastes like sour sweets in the sweet shop with extra sugar on them.
It sounds like the birds singing softly in the trees.
It feels like the soft pillow on my bed at night.
It lives with me in my home most of the time.

Laura Owen (10)
Ysgol Bethel, Caernarfon

Kindness

Kindness is a bird in the blue summer sky.
It smells like roses in the green grass field at springtime.
It tastes like Turkish delight just been made in the factory.
It sounds like newborn lambs crying for their mum.
It feels like pure air blowing in my face.
It looks like a huge chocolate fountain
It lives mostly in my heart.

Laura Jones (10)
Ysgol Bethel, Caernarfon

Luck

Luck is a flower that lives on the beach
And in my heart
And makes all my dreams come true.

It smells like nature all around
That makes me feel lucky to be alive
In the beautiful country fields.

It tastes like the greenest kiwi in the world
It's green like the grass that the wind blows one side
To another.

It sounds like the bluebirds that sing outside
On the green grass and trees above.

It feels like I could run forever and ever
And never come back.

It lives in my school, Bethel, where all the luck comes out.

Claudia Roberts (10)
Ysgol Bethel, Caernarfon

Coolness

Coolness is a chav
Chasing another Chelsea chav.
It smells like my lynx after my breakfast.
In the early morning.
It tastes like a bar of chocolate being left in the sun all week.
It sounds like my hamster moving in the night.
It is cool when I'm watching Everton winning at Goodison Park
The home of Everton.
Cool is the book I'm reading
And it's very cool.
It lives in the heart of a tough, popular, cool guy.

Guto Griffiths (9)
Ysgol Bethel, Caernarfon

My Mum

My mum is very kind
She works in Halo,
And makes chocolate bars
If I'm naughty she doesn't mind.

Natalie Thomas (8)
Ysgol Bryncrug, Tywyn

Sherwood Forest

S herwood Forest
H uge and old
E normous woods
R ustling leaves
W oods are dark
O ld and ancient
O ak tree standing
D ark and spooky.

F ar and deep
O wls will hoot
R iver babbling, splashing by
E normous branches filling the sky
S tars gleam in the night
T onight they shimmer and dance with the river.

Kayleigh Thomas (11)
Ysgol Bryncrug, Tywyn

Sherwood Forest

S herwood Forest
H uge and old,
E normous woods
R ustling leaves.
W oods are quiet
O ld and ancient,
O aks are standing,
D eep and silent.

F oxes scampering
O n leafy paths.
R abbits are hopping through
E very night as the big trees sleep.
S himmering shining stars look down
T o watch the river bubbling by.

Sophie Unsworth (10)
Ysgol Bryncrug, Tywyn

Sherwood Forest

Ancient forest
Dark and old.
Tall, thick, brown
Enormous trees.

Branches, twigs
With lots of leaves,
Green and rustling,
In the wind.

Squirrels scamper
On every branch,
The wild boar
Grunting down the path.

In the night
The sparkling stars
Shining, glistening
On the babbling stream.

Iwan Jones (10)
Ysgol Bryncrug, Tywyn

Sherwood Forest

S herwood Forest is very spooky
H uge old oak trees stand about.
E normous leafy green branches tall and thick
R ustling leaves crackle scattering the ground.
W oods are silent all the time.
O ld trees green and shady.
O ak tree standing with pride.
D ark secrets are deep inside.

F ar beneath the animals sleep
O wls hoot half the night,
R obin Hood comes night and day.
E very night the forest goes to bed.
S himmering water in the river splashing and bubbling,
T all trees standing strong always going on and on . . .

Ava MacPherson (10)
Ysgol Bryncrug, Tywyn

Sherwood Forest

S herwood Forest
H uge and old
E normous trees, tall and green
R ippling,sparkling great blue sky
W oods falling out of the sky
O ak trees
O ld and brown
D ark trees sleeping soundly.

F ar below animals play
O wls sleep most of the day
R ustling, scampering all around
E ach one on the ground
S tars look down on the bubbling stream
T onight it shimmers like a dream.

Alicia Crane (9)
Ysgol Bryncrug, Tywyn

Sherwood Forest

Ancient forest
Filled with oak trees.
Dark and leafy
Full of shadows.

Leaves green and brown
Fill the branches
With loads of sound,
Rustling, whispering in the wind.

Deep in the forest
Hear the grunting of the boar.
The scattering of many tiny feet
As animals scatter from his roar.

The river is babbling on its way
Rippling, splashing into rocks.
Fish jumping and swimming by,
As the sun shines up high in the sky.

Thomas Davies (11)
Ysgol Bryncrug, Tywyn

Skateboarding

Flying down the ramp
A cheetah at full speed
Thunder in my wheels.

A surfer riding the crib
Shooting through the air
A bullet from a gun
King of the world.

Rocks to fakey
A Ferrari in reverse
Wheels hook over the grinding pole
The thud of the board
Riding the pole
90 degree spin
Axle stall
Screeching, grinding metal on metal.

At one with my board
A peregrine falcon hunting its prey
The thrill of the chase.

The roller coaster ride of a lifetime.

Owen Cain (11)
Ysgol Cwm Y Glo, Caernarfon

Morning Madness!

Bacon sizzling,
Toast popping,
Milk pouring,
Juice squeezing,
Pancakes flipping,
Eggs frying,
Sausages banging,
Pots clanging,
Butter spreading,
Cereal crunching,
Mouths munching,
Crumbs falling,
Jam dripping,
Honey sticking,
Cats sneaking,
Mums rushing,
Babies dribbling,
Tea spilling,
Dad shouting,
'What a mess!'
Sister sulking,
Dishwasher loading,
Tables wiping,
Faces washing,
Pots cleaning,
Mops mopping,
Bags packing,
Dogs barking,
Kids dressing,
Hurry everybody!
Bus leaving!

Hannah Wilson (10)
Ysgol Cwm Y Glo, Caernarfon

Garden Of All Seasons

Birds sing in blossoming trees,
Chicks chirp in cosy nests.
Crocuses raise their dainty faces
To the warm light of day.
Daffodils stand proudly on parade,
New life emerging from the soft brown earth.

Scorching sun bathes the garden in a sea of colour.
Roses,
Poppies,
Sunflowers,
Lilies,
Cornflowers,
Dance in the swaying breeze,
Faces raised in worship.
Bees, busily buzz from blossom to blossom,
Whilst the lawn languishes, lazily.
A velvet blanket adorning the earth.

A merry brook gurgles and splashes over rocks,
Playing happily around the old oak tree.
Leaves like ginger ballerinas,
Pirouetting, twirling, floating
In a blaze of colour,
Onto the flaming carpeted ground.

Majestic beauty,
Snowflakes flutter silently, softly
Amongst delicately scattered snowdrops,
Blanketing the garden
Waiting for spring.

Emma Smith (10)
Ysgol Cwm Y Glo, Caernarfon

A Menu For Making Teachers Angry

Starter
Being late for school served with chucking your coat on the floor.
Throwing an apple core across the room in a sauce
                                of flicked rubbers.
Smudged work and rubbing out a bed of ink blots.

Main Course
Dancing on a table served with singing very loudly!
Being rude served with a light batter of bullying.
A room filled with children breaking wind sauteed with
Ripping up work coated with sticky fingers.
Eating at 11.30am mixed by spitting bits of food at other children.
Doing your work totally wrong coated in writing on the table.
Going to sleep in class on a bed of saying that the lessons
Are boooooooorrrrrrrring!

Dessert
A light stew of chewed up pencils with finely grated run out pens.
Sticking your chewing gum under the table dipped in shouting.
Not doing your homework mixed with writing fake absence excuses
                                to the teacher.

Osian Davies (10)
Ysgol Cwm Y Glo, Caernarfon

The Gym

Sweat dripping,
Pouring down my face,
Hands hot,
Scorching like desert sun,
Hungry,
Like a ravenous lion,
Energy drained,
Heart pumping,
Exhaustion!
Is this really healthy?

Katie Roberts (10)
Ysgol Cwm Y Glo, Caernarfon

Football

My black and white football
Flying,
Bending
Across the cloudy blue sky.
Swerving into the goal.
Yes!
Celebration!
Running down the pitch.
Supporters shouting, calling my name.
Wind pushing into my face!
Man of the match!

Dylan Jones (10)
Ysgol Cwm Y Glo, Caernarfon

Children Of Africa

The sound of children
Crying in starvation
Dusty tracks on tear-stained cheeks
Stomachs empty
Like a dark corner
In a lonely room
Throats as dry as the Sahara
Lack of water
Famished and ravenous
Longing for food
Neglected children
Begging for mercy
Children dying in poverty
No whispers of hope
Children dying from war.

Natasha Lowe-Sellers (11)
Ysgol Cwm Y Glo, Caernarfon

Pigs

Snuffling and snorting in the grimy grot
The foul stench of dung fills the air
Slimy swill pours from a bucket
Stinky siblings fight to the trough
Gluttonously gobbling
Selfishly scoffing
Ravenously rummaging
Gormandizingly guzzling
Barbarically battling in the bad-mannered bout
Mud fights in the mornings
Flinging the fetid filth back and forth like a ball in a
Game of tennis
Mud-bathing in the bog
Before snuggling up with Mum in the warm hay.

Conor Handy (10)
Ysgol Cwm Y Glo, Caernarfon

Big Brothers

Punching, head-locking and kicking,
They could be caring and generous!
Bossy and bad mannered,
They could be kind and courteous!
Lazy, selfish and sluggish,
They could be hardworking and helpful!
The smell of Lynx makes me wheezy,
Oh, how I wish they could be bright and breezy!

Patrick Griffith   (10)
Ysgol Cwm Y Glo, Caernarfon

The Rugby Six Nations Final

Big day today,
Millennium Stadium changing rooms,
Selected for Wales' first 15!
My dream's come true.
Warmed up and ready to go.
Coach shouting,
Players pumping,
Crowd roaring,
Anthem singing,
Hearts racing,
Whistle blowing,
Foot kicking,
Ball flying,
Fans screaming,
Props sweating,
Points scoring,
Wingers running,
Ground shaking,
Team winning,
Tears rolling down my cheeks,
Filled with elation,
Jubilant,
Triumphant,
Exhausted,
Electrified,
The trophy in the cabinet,
The Red Dragon victorious.

Jordan Lewis (11)
Ysgol Cwm Y Glo, Caernarfon

Imagination

The feeling of waking,
To a world of imagination
Inside an apple pie,
Eating your way through,
Swimming in cake,
Flying in the sky,
To the small world
On top of a tree,
Where birds fly in books.
A cat with two heads
Walks across the pink, red sea,
A running ball jogs through town.
I see Mars exercising
And a winged dog floats by.

Now that's imagination!

Aidan Christy (10)
Ysgol Cwm Y Glo, Caernarfon

Football Crazy

Bursting with pride as I pull on my Welsh shirt,
Walking through the tunnel to the pitch of childhood dreams;
The pressure of the final in my home country,
Like a ton weight on my heart.
Weak with nerves
Crowd calling, 'Come on Wales!'
Tears of joy prick at my eyes.
This moment will be remembered all of my life,
Ninety minutes that will stay with me forever.

Lloyd Hughes (11)
Ysgol Cwm Y Glo, Caernarfon

Mum

A face,
Sparkling, brown, beautiful eyes,
Rosy cheeks like the petals of a flower,
Kind, gentle, loving lips
Whisper comforting words
That warm me when I'm cold,
Filling me with happiness,
Kissing away the pain.
Delicate hands
Hugging away the sadness
Of my tears.
Helping and supporting my efforts.
Clearing and cleaning.
The mess I leave.
Fragrant rose,
Graceful swan,
Peaceful angel!

Cian Bierd-Hughes (10)
Ysgol Cwm Y Glo, Caernarfon

Wales

Magnificent majestic mountains
Towering over towns, lakes, woods
Crumbling rocks
Falling like marbles on a run
Gurgling and giggling brooks
Laughing and playing in sunlight like children.
The land where I was born
The land from which I grow
Where I shall lay to rest.

Jennifer Lyon-Jones (9)
Ysgol Cwm Y Glo, Caernarfon

Cat

Black and white
Smooth and sleek
Panther of the living room
Lazing in the sun
Sneaking p the stairs
Napping in my bed
Outstretched claws
Dreaming of hunting mice
Pouncing on his prey
Scratching
Biting
Tearing limb from limb
Playing with its murder victim
Carrying it to the house like a trophy

Cuddles, you're my best friend.

Hayley Hughes (11)
Ysgol Cwm Y Glo, Caernarfon

The Secret Garden!

Swans glide gracefully on a lily pond.
Birds sing in faraway trees
Animals all around.
Children, run in freedom
Waterfalls stream down a rock face
A torpedo of water shoots to the ground.
Scented flowers blossom amongst trees and bushes.
Horses gallop over bridges,
Lavender-coloured mountains tower in the distance
Happiness all around.
People stuck in mazes
Warm rain tumbles down
Bees and frogs on a swing.
The secrets of my garden.

Rebecca Parry (10)
Ysgol Cwm Y Glo, Caernarfon

Seaside

Summer,
Children swimming,
Playing, paddling and splashing in the rock pools.
Glistening waves,
Crashing and sweeping over their heads.
Aunties bulging out of bikinis,
Lying beneath the baking sun,
Waiting for their dull, white skin
To transform into the roasting red of sunburn.
The peeling tan!
Singing ice cream vans
Swerve onto the promenade,
Youngsters beg for money,
Can I have?
Can I have?
Can I have?
Mr Whippy slaving to make his fortune.
Fish and chip picnics
Waft on the air,
Amongst the salty sea breeze,
Our family on the beach.

Rebekha Owen (10)
Ysgol Cwm Y Glo, Caernarfon

My Dog

You're dirty
You bring in sticks.
You bark at nothing in particular.
You get all wet and I have to dry you!
Muddy paw prints on the carpet.
You smell like a dead fish!
You say you want food but don't eat it
But . . .

I wouldn't change you for the world.

Daniel Chetwode-Barton (10)
Ysgol Cwm Y Glo, Caernarfon

Cars

Speeding along on the motorway
On a sunny Saturday morning
Colourful cars
Stopping and starting
Smoke blowing from the exhaust
Poisoning the atmosphere
Fords
Ferraris
BMWs
Peugeots
Renaults
Subarus
Mitsubishis
Polluting the environment
Making people sick
Noisy
Rushing
Filthy,
Road hogs.

Liam Hughes (9)
Ysgol Cwm Y Glo, Caernarfon

The Wishing Well

I wish you friends,
I wish you love,
I wish you happiness from above
I wish you freedom and not one law.

I wish you peace,
I wish you rest,
I wish you fun,
I wish you patience,
I wish you tolerance,
I wish you a long life,
What could I wish you more?

Jasper Clough (9)
Ysgol Cwm Y Glo, Caernarfon

Freedom

Out on a sunny spring day
Running in freedom.
Hair soaring in the wind
Twirling around,
Dancing.
Free and independent.
Birds singing a merry tune,
Lambs hungrily bleating.
Running,
    Running,
Until I see a cliff.
Lying down I see the sea!
    Waves,
Lapping on the shore.
Seagulls floating,
Peace all around.
Dolphins leaping and diving
Into the glistening waves.
Kites hovering on the breeze,
Pinks,
    Blues,
        Oranges,
          Yellows,
A rainbow of colour across the sky.
Under the waves shimmering fish
Plunge out of sight,
Soothing sunset lower me down
Into soft dreams.

Holly Smith (8)
Ysgol Cwm Y Glo, Caernarfon

The Garden At Night

Peeping silently through my bedroom window,
Hungry fox cubs dash through the bushes
Hedgehogs scuttle amongst mountains of autumn leaves,
Badgers scavenge greedily for food.
Wind whistles a soothing tune,
Stars twinkle like diamonds
On a black velvet curtain
Lights dim as the music of the day fades.

Goodnight sweet garden.

Rebecca Wilson (9)
Ysgol Cwm Y Glo, Caernarfon

Happiness - Haiku

Blue and silver bike
Speeding, flying over ramps
King of suspension.

Gerallt Jones (8)
Ysgol Cwm Y Glo, Caernarfon

Raging Storm

People fishing for fish,
Everybody having a good time,
Before the storm,
Three people washed overboard,
People rush into the cabin,
Scared out of their wits.
Panicking!
Crying!
Screaming!
Terrified of the gigantic waves,
Crashing against the sides of the boat.
Lightning strikes the mast,
The boat capsizes,
Lives are lost.

Danny Cain (8)
Ysgol Cwm Y Glo, Caernarfon

Happiness

When I wake up in the morning
On a summer's day
I smell toast in the grill
As fresh as a cloud.
On the beach
The sun as hot as the
Burning flames of fire.
Seagulls flying like kites in the sky
Boats sail away to far-off lands.
Perfect!

Oisín Lowe-Sellers (8)
Ysgol Cwm Y Glo, Caernarfon

Happiness All Day And Night

Sunday morning,
A new day ahead,
The birds flying in the sky above.
Draw the curtains,
Look outside,
See the children laughing
With joy in their eyes.
Downstairs, breakfast is ready.
Go to the park,
At lunchtime,
Let's go to the chippy for a treat!'
The ice cream van,
'Does anyone want an ice cream?'
Tea time,
I'm going to the café.
As darkness closes in
It's time to go home.
Resting in the armchair,
Singing songs as I flow.
Bedtime,
Where's my teddy?'
Ah, there underneath my bed,
Night night,
I'm going to bed with my ted.

Lilac Amor (8)
Ysgol Cwm Y Glo, Caernarfon

Trees

Trees are big and some trees are small
They grow everywhere
Some grow straight and some grow tall
Every tree gives us oxygen
There are hundreds of different kinds of trees.

Christopher Hulme (9)
Ysgol Cwm Y Glo, Caernarfon

Happiness

Birds singing in the morning
My sister puts on her make-up
As I come down the stairs I smell toast.
It's a hot day today, Dad's going to work
Me and my friend away on our bikes.
Long hot days in the countryside,
Picnics at the river, ice cream and fizzy drinks.

Chloe Jones (9)
Ysgol Cwm Y Glo, Caernarfon

Fairies

In my bedroom was a fairy
Standing on my shelf
She was all alone and thirsty
Blonde hair curly
Framing her pretty face
Her purple dress floating in the breeze
Delicate
Beautiful wings.

Fern Coxhead (8)
Ysgol Cwm Y Glo, Caernarfon

.

Happiness

Sunrise on a summer's day
Birds singing merrily
A joyful tune.
The smell of home-made bread
Wafting through the house.
The smell of bacon sizzling under the grill.
Toast burning under the sun.
Colours of the rainbow fill the world.

Matthew Roberts (8)
Ysgol Cwm Y Glo, Caernarfon

Happiness

Sunrise on a summer's day
Birds singing merrily a joyful tune
The smell of lovely baked toast
With butter spread on the toast.

Mum humming, happy birthday
The smell of toast wafting through the house.

Sion Roberts (8)
Ysgol Cwm Y Glo, Caernarfon

Happiness in The Morning

On a Sunday morning opening the curtains
Listening to the church bells going *ding-dong*.
Watching the church people going into church
Look at the clock, it's time to get up.

Going downstairs settling into hot toast.
Sit on the sofa listen to sad press.
Cheer up people!
God is answering.

Church people cheering to the answers of God.
Going to the park, here comes the ice cream man.
'Who wants an ice cream?'
'Me! Me! Me!'
Shout the children.

I better go home it's time for lunch
Yum-yum ham sandwiches.
See the church people coming out of church.
With big Bibles in the hands of church people.

I've finished lunch.
I'm going to watch TV now.

Corrina Knight (9)
Ysgol Cwm Y Glo, Caernarfon

Summertime

As you wake up in the morning
And see the flowers open.
Seeing the colours of summer
Red, blue, purple, pink and yellow and
Listen to the song of breeze.
The sun is shining, and the birds are singing.
While getting on my slippers and creeping down
The stairs and into the garden.
I can hear the birds calling good morning
To the world.

Danielle Lynden (8)
Ysgol Cwm Y Glo, Caernarfon

Happiness

Birds singing in the trees.
Dad reading a newspaper.
Mum cooking eggs.
My sister moaning.
My brother playing football.
Chloe coming to call.
Endless hours of playing.

Shannon Christy (8)
Ysgol Cwm Y Glo, Caernarfon

Tractor

Tractor working in the fields
Feeding the cows
Ploughing the land
Planting the seeds
Herding the sheep
The farmer's best friend.

Matthew Hughes (9)
Ysgol Cwm Y Glo, Caernarfon

Snakes

S nakes live in Asia and Africa.
N ervous feelings created by snakes in case of attack.
A snake can be poisonous and can
K ill people.
E lectrifying, petrifying, terrifying,
S nakes can land on sea, rivers and streams.

Daniel Land (8)
Ysgol Cwm Y Glo, Caernarfon

Branwen's War

The war was horrible in the night.
I heard a scream.
When I wcnt out I saw blood.
It looked like lava.
My uncle was dead.
It felt like someone had slapped me.

Adam Thomas (9)
Ysgol Gynradd Bodedern, Holyhead

Branwen's War

Out in the war,
Blood everywhere.
The noise -
Clattering, crashing,
People in pain,
On the floor.
I'm scared
Someone will kill me.
I'm crying.

Blood everywhere,
People dying.
Black like night,
Red like fire,
Colours of war.
Bodies on the floor.
People shouting and screaming.
I don't want another war.
The country is destroyed.

Elen Jones (8)
Ysgol Gynradd Bodedern, Holyhead

Branwen's War

Branwen hates war
Hearing the sword slicing.
Here she is in pain
And nothing to do.

Branwen is imagining
What will happen.
War!
Everybody fighting,
Slicing their heads off.

Branwen thinks
What will happen
To her brother.
Imagines that he is going to die.
Will he be . . .
Burnt,
Stabbed,
Slashed,
Destroyed?
Then finding him
In the mud
Dark fire around him
And dead people around him too.
It is Hell.

Daniel Owen (10)
Ysgol Gynradd Bodedern, Holyhead

Branwen's War

Burning fire everywhere
People screaming and screaming
Screaming, 'Help!'
People covered in blood.
People I hate,
People I hate
Who fight like
Wild animals.

I hate
I hate the war
The most horrible thing I have ever seen,
Blood!
Blood!
Everywhere I go
The blood is red like the sea.

Everywhere I go
The people are dead
Blood on the floor
I am frightened
Oh poor country!

Leah Edwards (9)
Ysgol Gynradd Bodedern, Holyhead

Branwen's War

Burning fire everywhere,
People crying, crying, crying.
Armies fighting and swords clattering,
Blood everywhere.
Everyone screaming and shooting,
The noise and armies, I was scared.

The bodies on the floor
Smoke everywhere in the sky.
The mud on the floor,
People dying.
The armies destroying
Hoof prints on the ground
It was scary, very, very scared,
It was all the army's fault.

Shannon Hughes (9)
Ysgol Gynradd Bodedern, Holyhead

Branwen's War

Everyone crying and blood everywhere,
People fighting and screaming,
People killed, that horrible pain.

There is fire everywhere,
Smoke with ugly smell,
Red blood like water,
People shouting,
The war was terrifying.

John Jones (8)
Ysgol Gynradd Bodedern, Holyhead

Branwen's War

People shouting and running away
From the red-hot fire.
Enemies falling on top of us,
People crying,
'Help, help,' said the children.

'We should go to fight,' said the men,
And off they went to the war.
Bang, crash, clatter,
The blood like a river,
The people crying like water.

Catrin Jones (9)
Ysgol Gynradd Bodedern, Holyhead

Rosie And Sally

Rosie and Sally bark at the door,
When somebody's at the door they bark.
I open the door,
They bark louder,
But when I close the door,
They stop barking,
Instead they sleep.

My Rosie and Sally are bad girls sometimes,
But my dogs are good girls really.

Aron Pritchard (10)
Ysgol Gynradd Bodedern, Holyhead

Robin Hood

Robin Hood goes here and there
He goes everywhere
He can't stop going on his horse
Clip clop, goes on his horse everywhere.
Clip clop, going here and there.

He's great and he's kind, he steals from the rich
And gives to the poor.
Robin Hood.

Billy Jones (9)
Ysgol Gynradd Bodedern, Holyhead

Branwen's War

The smile dead
The garden all dried up
Soldiers fighting, screaming.

The sun of happiness gone
The moon of war coming
Branwen in the shadows.

The blue sky turned black
The black clouds entered the sky
The sky overthrown by darkness.

Deiniol Huws (10)
Ysgol Gynradd Bodedern, Holyhead

The Mallard

The Mallard, it is fast,
But will its speed last?

It is blue.
It zoomed round the track,
Like a boy running to the loo!

It zoomed through the station,
Without losing acceleration.

It reaches 126mph
What a lot of power!

Remember the Mallard is a bird,
But this poem is about a train!

Jacob Morgan (9)
Ysgol Gynradd Llanegryn, Tywyn

The Concorde

A gigantic white plane,
It goes so fast it's insane.

The big wings are pointy,
Like green shining holly.

The dangerous hot rockets,
Would never fit in your pockets!

It is very spiky at the front,
It can do a brilliant stunt.

Fast as a leopard it goes
But in the air the Concorde flows.

Rhys Roberts (9)
Ysgol Gynradd Llanegryn, Tywyn

Speed

Vroom, vroom,
300mph engine,
6,000 brake horsepower,
5 gallon oil tank,
Speeding round the corner,
Climbing the speedometer,
Broke the world record!

George Wall (9)
Ysgol Gynradd Llanegryn, Tywyn

The Fastest Speedboat

Fast speedboat
On waving water,
Stops
On soft sand.
I go in the water.
Once again I'm on the boat.
It feels fantastic.

Dewi Pugh (10)
Ysgol Gynradd Llanegryn, Tywyn

The Dog

I went to the park with my dog.
He was as happy as a frog.
When I threw the ball
He brought it back.
I gave him a treat
After his meat.
I went to town, I bought a new lead,
I took him home, dog went to his bed
And into a new dream.

Laura Wright (8)
Ysgol Gynradd Llanegryn, Tywyn

The Trip To The Football Match

On my way to football,
It was pouring down with rain.
I went to the train station,
I was on my way to Spain.

It was Scotland vs Spain,
I was playing for Scotland.

I felt I was in sincere pain,
It was 12 o'clock,
I fell asleep and gave my brain a 8-hour break,
I went to the shop,
I bought some pop
And then I was in Spain, ready to play my game.

Jordan Rodgers (10)
Ysgol Gynradd Llanegryn, Tywyn

The Fastest Bird

It's small in the air but
Big on the ground,
It has two big propellers
And likes to fly around.

Taxiing now it's very slow,
But not as slow as a snail!
It's as fast as a leopard
In the air.

It's very, very popular,
It was the first one ever.

Eirug Roberts (9)
Ysgol Gynradd Llanegryn, Tywyn

The Journey

I went into my mum's cupboard to hide
I fell through the wall and saw a tide.
I saw a shop so I went in,
I saw someone in a spin.
I was confused.
I tried to find clues.
I made a friend, we went home,
We heard my mum's tone!
We had tea.
In the end we went to bed.

Nia Morris (8)
Ysgol Gynradd Llanegryn, Tywyn

Cookie The Horse

My horse is huge, furry and brown,
I am going to ride it, right into town.
I'll get the saddle, bridle and reins,
We are going to the shop, that's our aim.

She'll run up the field through the gates,
Down the lane to see her horse mates,
On the way we'll see flowers and trees,
We'll go through the woods and feel the breeze.

When we come out of the trees,
We see a group of big bees!
On the path we see three cyclists on bikes
They are going up the hill to take a hike!

And then a car comes whizzing past,
The wheels are spinning, gosh that's fast!
We finally reach the shop with the food
But the person at the till was surely in a mood!

On the way back we go exactly the same way
But the place we go past looks like Colwyn Bay!

Ella Morgan (8)
Ysgol Gynradd Llanegryn, Tywyn

Spitfire

(In memory of my great grandad)

The fields and houses down below
Look a bit like home
But this trip is no holiday
He's in his plane alone.

He gets the shout to drop the bombs
He'll do his duty well,
Smoke and fire down on Earth
Destruction, death and hell.

Then he sees the German planes
Approaching from behind,
Gunfire, blood, a flash of light,
His eyes, his eyes, he's blind.

The children on the ground below
Laugh, shout and play
Not seeing the brave pilot
Who replays that fateful day.
. . . Forever
. . . and ever
. . . and ever.

Robert Jervis (9)
Ysgol Gynradd Llanegryn, Tywyn

My Bike

My blue and yellow bike,
Has big wheels.

It came from Mrs Davies
Mountain bike.

I keep it in the barn or outside.
I met my friend Sam
On the road to church.

Matthew Wood (8)
Ysgol Gynradd Llanegryn, Tywyn

Journey Through Town

Cars rush in the street,
People have something to eat.
Some towns are big, some towns are not.
Some towns have parks,
Some towns do not.
When it's winter, every shop's roof is white.
Bikes wobble through town
To the shop before it closes.

Tomos Williams (7)
Ysgol Gynradd Llanegryn, Tywyn

Walking The Dog

I went into town,
The dog was brown.
I frowned at the girl with a crown.
I saw Ella in town,
She had bought a crown.
The lead was red,
Like a duvet cover on a bed.
I went into the shop
And I bought a mop.
I had my perm,
And saw a worm.
We played in the park with a ball,
The ball had come from the mall.
I went to my nan's for an hour,
And I had a shower.
We went to our beds,
And rested our heads.
  Annie and the dog, Patch.

Annie Evans (9)
Ysgol Gynradd Llanegryn, Tywyn

The Winter Weather

The spiky, cold, smooth holly
The snowy, crunchy, messy cold snow
The spiky, smooth hat.
The smooth, gentle snowman,
The freezing ice,
The spiky, cold icicle,
The smooth robin
The crunchy, slippy ice.

Nathaniel Sanllehi (7)
Ysgol Penmorfa, Prestatyn

The Winter Weather

The icicles are cold and shiny,
The cold white snow falls from the trees.
The cold winter weather freezes me fast.
The cold ice is freezing, slippy and white.
The cold, icy snow freezes the cars.
The robins sing softly in the trees.
The cold ice is melting, melting fast.
The fluffy white snow falls to the ground.

Eden O'Shea-Price (7)
Ysgol Penmorfa, Prestatyn

What's It Like?

One, two, three,
What can I see?
The huge, red dragon
And it's snarling at me.

One, two, three,
What can I see?
The wet, strong, whale
And it's squirting water at me.

One, two, three,
What can I see?
The dark blue sea
And it's splashing me.

One, two, three,
What can I see?
A big, fat elephant
And it's stomping me.

One, two, three,
What can I see?
The wet drippy rain
And it's soaking me.

One, two, three,
What can I see?
A fluffy, white lamb
And it's smiling at me.

One, two, three,
What can I see?
A juicy red apple
And it's making me hungry.

Robin Back (7)
Ysgol Penmorfa, Prestatyn